Bedtime Bible

Bedtime Bible

Stephanie Jeffs

Illustrated by Graham Round

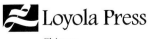
Loyola Press

Chicago

Loyola Press

3441 North Ashland Avenue
Chicago, Illinois 60657

© 1999 AD Publishing Services Ltd
1 Churchgates, The Wilderness, Berkhamsted, Herts HP4 2UB
Illustrations © 1999 Graham Round

All rights reserved. No part of this publication may be reproduced, stored in a retrieval system, or
transmitted, in any form or by any means, electronic, mechanical, photocopying, recording, or otherwise,
without the prior written permission of the publishers.

Published in Great Britain by Marshall Pickering, an imprint of HarperCollins

ISBN 0-8294-1428-2
Printed and bound in Singapore
99 00 01 02 03 / 10 9 8 7 6 5 4 3 2 1

A Word to Parents and Grandparents

Through countless generations, parents and grandparents have told and read Bible stories to their children. This collection of forty-two stories and prayers is for sharing with preschoolers at naptime and bedtime, when assurances of God's love and care are especially comforting.

Introduce your little ones to the great heroes of the faith—Adam and Eve, Abraham and Sarah, Mary and Joseph, Jesus and his friends. Pray with them the simple prayers. Tuck them in bed, knowing that they are in God's hands.

Contents

The Beautiful Garden

In the beginning, the earth was empty and dark and quiet. Only God was there.

Then God spoke. "Let there be light," God said.

God made the light and the darkness, the big, tall mountains, and the deep blue seas. God filled the land with plants and flowers and trees.

God made the round, spinning earth, the red-hot sun,

and the silvery moon. God made the planets and the twinkling stars.

Then God filled the seas with slippery, shiny fish, the air with birds that chatter and sing, and the land with animals that leap and crawl.

God looked at the brand-new earth, and God was pleased. It was very good.

"Now I will make some people," God said. "They will be like me. They will take care of the earth."

So God made Adam and Eve.

God loved Adam and Eve very much. God wanted them to enjoy the earth and to be happy. God gave them a beautiful garden to live in. It was called the Garden of Eden.

Thank you, God, for the beautiful world you have given me!

The Serpent in the Garden

Adam and Eve were happy. Friendly animals lived in the garden, and Adam and Eve chose names for them.

Delicious fruits and vegetables grew in the garden, and Adam and Eve tasted them all—all except the fruit from the tree in the middle of the garden. "Don't eat any fruit from that tree," God told them. "Don't even touch it."

One day a serpent came into the garden. It crept up to Eve and hissed in her ear. "God lied to you about the tree," the serpent said. "Go ahead and eat the fruit. It will make you wise, just like God!"

Eve looked at the fruit. It was ripe and juicy. She reached out and touched it. She took a big, deep bite. She gave some fruit to Adam.

Suddenly Adam and Eve were scared. What would

happen to them now?

"You disobeyed me and ate fruit from the tree in the middle of the garden," God said sadly. "Now you will have to leave the garden. You will have to go where animals are fierce and food is hard to get."

Adam and Eve cried as they left the beautiful garden. They wished they had never listened to the serpent. They wished they had obeyed God.

Dear God, I'm sorry I sometimes do things that are wrong. I need your help to do good.

Noah Builds a Boat

After Adam and Eve left the Garden of Eden, the world became an unhappy place. Most people forgot all about God. They fought all the time. They hurt each other.

God saw what was happening in the world, and God was very sad. "Why did I make the world?" God wondered.

There was just one person in the whole world who made God happy. Noah obeyed God. He treated other people kindly.

One day God spoke to Noah. "I wish I had never made the world," God said. "I am going to start all over again. I am going to flood the earth with water and wash it clean."

God told Noah to build a very big boat. God told him exactly how it should be made. So Noah cut down trees and made boards. He pounded pegs and hung doors. Finally he covered the bottom of the boat with thick, sticky tar to keep the water out.

Everyone thought Noah was crazy. "He's building a boat on dry land!" they said. They would not listen when Noah told them what God was going to do.

God told Noah to take every kind of animal with him into the boat. "Take your family with you too," God said. "I will save you all from the big flood."

Rain, Rain, and More Rain

The sky was turning dark. Noah and his family and all the animals were safely inside the big boat. Nobody else wanted to go into the boat, so God shut the door.

Drip! Drip! It began to rain.

Pitter-patter! The rain fell harder.

Gurgle! Splash! The rivers burst their banks and the seas flooded the land.

Soon Noah's boat was floating on the water. The rain continued for forty days until water covered everything in the whole world. But everyone inside the boat was safe and dry.

After many months, God sent a wind. The waters began to go down.

Noah took a raven from inside the boat and set it free. It flew back and forth, but it could not find dry land.

Then Noah took a
dove from inside the boat
and set it free. But the dove
came back, because there was still no
dry land.

Noah sent out the dove again. This time it came back
carrying an olive leaf.

A few days later God told Noah to leave the boat.
The animals slithered and crawled, leaped and ran onto
the dry land.

"Thank you, God, for keeping us safe!" said Noah.

Noah looked up and saw a huge rainbow.

"Look at the rainbow," God said. "It is a sign of my
promise: I will never again destroy the earth with a
flood."

*Thank you for
keeping Noah and
his family safe.
Thank you for
keeping me and my
family safe too.*

Abram's Journey

Abram was a rich man. He lived with his wife, Sarai, and their parents and cousins and aunts and uncles in the city of Haran.

One day God spoke to Abram. "Leave your home and your parents, your cousins and your aunts and uncles," God said. "I will lead you to a new land. I will make you the head of a great family. I will bless you. And one day everyone in the world will be blessed because of you."

Abram went to find Sarai. "We must pack up all our things and go where God leads us," he told her. So Abram and Sarai, with their servants and their sheep and their goats, set off.

They walked and walked. Each night they stopped and camped in their tents.

They did not know where they were going. But they knew that God had promised to be with them wherever they went.

It was a long, long journey.

At last they reached Canaan. All around them, as far as Abram and Sarai could see, was rich, beautiful farmland.

"This is the land I will give to you and your children," God said.

Thank you for being with me wherever I go.

A Gift from God

Abram and Sarai were getting old. They did not have any children, and this made them sad.

One day Abram and God were talking.

"I will take care of you," God promised. "I will give you more than you can imagine!"

"What I really want is a son," Abram told God. "And now we're too old to have children."

"I promise that you will have a son of your very own," God said. "Look up at the sky."

Abram looked up. He saw millions of twinkling stars.

"Can you count the stars?" God asked.

Abram shook his head.

"Your family will be as big as the number of stars," God said. "And I am going to give you new names. From now on, you will be Abraham, and your wife will be Sarah."

Some time later, Abraham and Sarah had a baby boy. They named him Isaac.

They knew that Isaac was a gift from God. They knew that God always keeps promises.

Thank you for always keeping your promises.

21

Jacob Plays a Trick

Isaac grew up and married Rebekah. They had two sons, Esau and Jacob. Even though the boys were twins, they were very different.

Esau was the firstborn. He liked to hunt. His skin was hairy. Isaac loved Esau more than Jacob.

Jacob liked to stay at home. He was a good cook. His skin was smooth. Rebekah loved Jacob more than Esau.

When Isaac was an old man and nearly blind, he wanted to give Esau a blessing.

"Before I bless you, go and get some of my favorite meat," Isaac said. So Esau went out hunting.

Rebekah did not want Isaac to bless Esau. "Quick!" she said to Jacob. "Pretend to be Esau. Dress yourself in his clothes. Wrap some animal skins around your arms, so they will feel hairy. I will make your father's favorite meal, and you can take it to him. Your father will never know, and you will get the blessing!"

Jacob did what Rebekah said. He took the food and went to see his father.

"Is that really you, Esau?" Isaac asked.

"Yes, Father," Jacob lied. Isaac reached out and touched the animal skins.

They felt just like Esau's hairy arms. And so Isaac blessed Jacob instead of Esau.

When Esau learned what Jacob had done, he decided to kill his brother. "You must run away," Isaac told Jacob. And Jacob did.

Joseph's Jealous Brothers

Jacob had a big family. He had twelve sons and one daughter. He loved his young son, Joseph, best of all.

Jacob gave Joseph a beautiful, bright coat. Joseph was pleased. He wore his new coat as often as he could. He liked to show it off.

Joseph's big brothers were jealous. They saw how much their father loved Joseph. They did not like Joseph's new coat. They did not like Joseph either.

While Joseph's big brothers took care of their father's sheep, Joseph stayed home. One day Jacob said to Joseph, "Go and see how your brothers are doing." So Joseph set off, wearing his wonderful coat. His brothers saw him coming.

"Here comes Joseph," one of them said with a groan.

"I've had enough of him," said another.

"Let's kill him!" said a third. "No one will know. We could say he's been eaten by a wild animal."

"No," said big brother Reuben.

"Don't kill him. Put him in this empty well." Reuben planned to rescue Joseph later.

As soon as Joseph got near, his brothers grabbed him. They tore off his beautiful coat and threw him into the well.

At the bottom of the well, Joseph had lots of time to think. He did not know what his brothers might do. He did not know that God was watching over him.

But God was with Joseph, even in the well. God had big plans for him.

A Slave in Egypt

Poor Joseph! His brothers had taken his wonderful coat. They had thrown him into a well. Then they sat down to eat.

"Look!" said Judah. In the distance they saw a long line of people and camels on their way to Egypt.

"I have a good idea," said Judah. "Let's sell Joseph to those people. They will take him to Egypt to be a slave."

The brothers laughed and agreed. What a great way to get rid of their braggy little brother!

As soon as the people came near, the brothers pulled Joseph out of the well. They sold him for twenty silver coins. Then they ripped his coat, dipped it in goat's

blood, and went back home.

"Look what we found!" they said to their father, showing him the coat.

Jacob saw the blood on the coat. "My son has been killed by a wild animal!" he cried. For many days, Jacob wept for Joseph. Nobody could comfort him.

Jacob did not know that Joseph was safe and well in Egypt. He did not know that someday Joseph would be a great ruler. Joseph would bring his brothers and his father to live with him in Egypt. He would give them food and land. Then Jacob would be happy again.

Dear God, help me to know you are with me, especially when I'm scared.

The Baby in the Basket

God's people, the Israelites, lived in Egypt. It was not their own country, and they wanted to go home. But they were slaves, and they could not escape.

One day the Egyptian king had a horrible idea.

"We will kill all their baby boys," he said.

An Israelite mother had a baby boy. She kept him in her house to hide him from the Egyptians.

The baby grew and grew. He chuckled and gurgled. He wriggled and kicked. He made more and more noise.

"I cannot hide him any longer!" said the mother. She made a waterproof basket and put her baby in it. Then she hid the basket in the reeds by the river Nile. The baby's sister, Miriam, watched and waited to see what would happen.

An Egyptian princess came to the river to bathe. She saw the basket. She heard crying. She opened the basket and found the baby.

"Don't cry," she said. "I will take care of you. I will call you Moses."

"I know someone who can help you!" said Miriam.

She ran to find her mother.

"Take care of baby Moses," said the princess to his mother. "When he is old enough, he can come to live with me at the palace."

Let My People Go

The Israelites were slaves in Egypt. They had to work hard all day, making bricks in the hot sun. They wished they could leave Egypt and go to their own land.

One day God said to Moses, "My people are unhappy. I want you to tell the king of Egypt to let them go!"

Moses was scared of the king. But he went to see him anyway. "God wants you to let the Israelites go!" said Moses bravely.

The king said, "No!"

Moses hit the river Nile with his shepherd's stick. The water turned red, like blood. "Let God's people go!" said Moses.

The king said, "No!"

Suddenly there were frogs in the food, frogs in the houses, frogs in the beds! "Let us go, or worse things will happen!" said Moses.

The king said, "No!"

Soon the land of Egypt was covered with biting gnats, then swarms of flies. All the cows got sick and died, and the people got painful boils on their skin. Hail fell like stones from the sky, and locusts ate all the crops. Finally, thick darkness covered Egypt. People could not see each other. They could not leave their houses.

"All right," said the king. "You can go!" But as the darkness lifted, the king changed his mind. "I will never let you go!" he said.

Thank you for protecting your people.

31

The Great Escape

Nine times, Moses asked the king of Egypt to let the Israelites go. Nine times, the king of Egypt said, "No!"

Once again, God spoke to Moses. "Tell my people to get ready," God said. "Tonight the king will beg them to leave."

The Israelites packed their bags. They put on their shoes and coats. They ate a quick supper of roasted lamb and flat bread. God told them to paint their doorposts with the lamb's blood. This was a sign, God said, that would keep them safe.

At midnight something terrible happened. In every Egyptian house, the firstborn children died. Even the king's son died.

The king of Egypt sent for Moses. "Take God's people, and go!" he shouted.

The Israelites left at once. But they had not gone far when the king changed his mind again. "Who will work for us now?" he said. "Get the chariots ready. We'll bring them back."

The Israelites could see the Red Sea in front of them. Suddenly they heard galloping hooves and clattering wheels behind them. They were trapped! What could they do?

"Don't be afraid," said Moses. "God is with us."

Moses stretched out his hand across the water. A strong wind began to blow. The waters parted to make a path. The Israelites stepped onto the path and walked across the sea on dry land. Then the waters came back together. God's people were safe.

Thank you for letting your people go.

33

Joshua and the Battle of Jericho

The city of Jericho had high stone walls with huge wooden gates. The gates were tightly shut, and all the people of Jericho were inside. No one went out, and no one came in.

The people of Jericho were frightened. Everyone had heard about the Israelites' great escape from Egypt. And everyone knew that God had promised to give Jericho to the Israelites.

But the Israelites were doing a strange thing.

Each day Joshua, their leader, and seven priests marched once around the city. The Israelite army marched behind them. As they marched, they blew

34

trumpets. They did this for six days.

On the seventh day, Joshua, the seven priests, and the army marched around the city seven times as the trumpets sounded. The people of Jericho whispered to each other, "What is going to happen?"

Suddenly Joshua cried out, "Shout! For God has given us the city of Jericho!"

The priests and soldiers shouted. The trumpeters blew harder. The walls of Jericho cracked and crumbled, wobbled and shook until they crashed to the ground.

The Israelites rushed into the city. God had given Jericho to them, just as God had promised.

> Dear God, I am glad you are stronger than the walls of Jericho.

Samuel's Sleepless Night

Hannah prayed for a baby. God answered her prayers, and baby Samuel was born.

When Samuel was old enough, Hannah took him to live at God's temple. Eli, the priest, looked after him and taught him about God.

One night Samuel suddenly woke up. "Samuel!" a voice had said.

Samuel opened his eyes. The room was almost dark. Eli was asleep in another room. Everything was quiet and still.

Samuel threw back his bedcovers and got up. He ran into Eli's room.

"Here I am," he said. "You called me."

"No I didn't," said Eli. "Go back to sleep."

Samuel lay down. He tried to go to sleep.

"Samuel!" the voice said again. Samuel ran back to Eli.

"I didn't call you," said Eli. "Go back to sleep."

"Samuel!" said the voice a third time. Again Samuel rushed to Eli.

Suddenly Eli knew who was calling Samuel. "God wants to speak to you," he said. "If you hear him again, say, 'Speak to me, Lord. I'm listening.'"

Samuel went back to bed.

"Samuel! Samuel!" said the voice.

Samuel took a deep breath. "Speak to me, Lord," he said. "I'm listening."

From that day on, God often spoke to Samuel. God gave Samuel messages for the Israelites.

> *Thank you for speaking to children. Help me to know what you are saying to me.*

The Shepherd Boy

David was a shepherd boy. He lived with his father, Jesse, and his seven brothers. David's brothers were big and strong. They were tall and handsome. They were all older than David.

David looked after his father's sheep. Sometimes he frightened away lions or bears that came to steal lambs. Sometimes he killed them with stones he threw from his sling.

One day God spoke to the prophet Samuel.

"Go to Bethlehem," said God. "I have chosen one of Jesse's sons to be the next king of Israel."

Samuel went to Jesse's house. He saw Jesse's oldest son. He was tall and handsome. "He would make a good king," thought Samuel.

But God said, "You see only what he looks like. I know what is in his heart. He is not the one."

Then Samuel saw Jesse's second son. He was big and strong. "He would make a good king," thought Samuel.

But God said, "He is not the one."

Samuel met all seven of Jesse's sons. All of them were big and handsome, tall and strong. But God had not chosen any of them to be king.

"Do you have any more sons?" Samuel asked Jesse.

"Just one," said Jesse. "My youngest boy is looking after my sheep."

When David arrived, God said to Samuel, "He's the one! David is still young, but I know his heart. I have chosen David to be king."

Samuel poured oil over David's head, and God's Spirit came to be with him.

Thank you for knowing what is in my heart.

David and the Giant

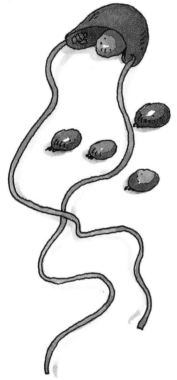

The Israelite soldiers were scared. A giant wanted to fight them.

Goliath had big strong arms and big strong legs and a big loud voice. And he carried a big sharp sword.

Every morning Goliath went to the Israelite soldiers. He took a big deep breath and shouted, "Who will come and fight me?"

Nobody wanted to fight Goliath. He was much too fierce and much too big.

One day David came to the Israelite camp to see his brothers, who were soldiers. When he heard about Goliath, he was angry. "We shouldn't be scared," he said. "God is on our side!"

So David went to the king. "I will fight Goliath," he said. "I don't need a sword or armor. All I need is my sling and five smooth stones."

"Come here!" roared Goliath when he saw David.

"You have a big sharp sword," David said. "But the living God is with me!"

Goliath stepped forward. David quickly put a stone in his sling. He whirled it around and around. The stone flew through the air and landed right in the middle of Goliath's forehead.

The giant crashed to the ground. The Israelite soldiers shouted for joy. Goliath was dead, and they did not have to be scared anymore.

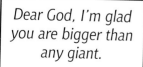

Dear God, I'm glad you are bigger than any giant.

40

God Takes Care of Elijah

Elijah was a prophet. He gave the Israelites messages from God.

The Israelites' land was very dry. The rivers ran out of water, and the plants in the fields dried up. There was nothing to eat and nothing to drink. It had not rained for a long time.

"Don't worry," said God to Elijah. "I will take care of you."

God told Elijah where to find a stream. Now he had plenty to drink. Some big birds brought Elijah food every morning and evening. Now he had plenty to eat.

But one day the stream dried up.

"Don't worry," said God to Elijah. "I will take care of you."

God told Elijah where to find a woman who would help him.

"Please give me something to eat," he asked her.

"I have only enough for one meal," said the woman.

42

"I am going to eat it with my son."

"God will take care of you," said Elijah. "Please share your food with me."

The woman took Elijah to her house. She used the last handful of flour. She poured out the last drops of oil.

Then the woman looked again. The jar was full of flour! The jug was brimming with oil! She could make lots more bread.

"God is taking care of you," said Elijah. "You will always have something to eat!"

Thank you for giving us our food.

43

Fire from Heaven

King Ahab and Queen Jezebel did not care about the living God. They worshiped Baal instead. Soon many other Israelites forgot about God and began to worship Baal too.

God sent the prophet Elijah to Ahab and Jezebel.

"What do you want?" Ahab asked crossly.

"I want a contest," said Elijah, "between my God and yours. If Baal wins, we will all worship Baal. If God wins, we will all worship God."

So Ahab and Jezebel and all the prophets of Baal went with Elijah to the top of a high mountain.

"We will build altars," said Elijah. "We will ask God and Baal to send down fire."

"Send down fire!" shouted the prophets of Baal. Nothing happened. The prophets danced around the altar. "Please send down fire!" they cried. No fire came, not even a puff of smoke.

"Perhaps Baal is asleep," said Elijah. He stepped up to God's altar. He put an offering on it. He poured water over it three times. And then Elijah prayed, "God of Abraham, Isaac, and Jacob, please show that you are the living God!"

Suddenly fire came down from heaven. It burned up the offering. It burned up the stones of the altar. It even burned up the water.

Everyone fell to the ground. "Elijah's God is the living God," they said.

> You are great and powerful, God. I love you.

45

Naaman and the Little Servant Girl

Everyone liked Naaman. He was a very brave soldier. But Naaman was sad. He had ugly white spots on his body. Soon nobody wanted to go near him. Everybody was afraid they might get spots too.

Naaman's wife had a little Israelite servant girl. "If Naaman could go to my country to see the prophet Elisha," the little girl said, "Elisha could make Naaman better."

So Naaman went to Israel to see Elisha. He knocked on Elisha's door. Elisha's servant came out and gave him a message: "Elisha says you should wash seven times in the river Jordan."

Naaman was angry. He did not want to wash in an Israelite river. "This is silly," Naaman thought. "I wanted Elisha to speak to me himself. I wanted him to touch the spots and make them go away. I might as well have stayed home and washed in one of our own rivers!"

"Excuse me, sir," said one of Naaman's servants. "If Elisha had asked you to do something hard, you would have done it. Why don't you try what he says?"

So Naaman went down to the river. He washed once. He washed twice. He washed three, four, five, and six times. Water went everywhere. But the spots were still there.

Naaman washed for the seventh time in the Jordan. This time the spots disappeared.

Naaman was happy. "Now I know," he said, "that there is only one true God—the God of Israel."

Dear God, show me how I can help other people just as the little girl helped Naaman.

Daniel in the Lions' Den

Daniel was a good man who loved God. He lived in Babylon, far from his home.

Daniel was honest and worked hard. One day the king said, "I am going to put you in charge of my kingdom."

But some bad men who lived in Babylon did not want Daniel in charge. They grumbled and complained. They tried to get Daniel in trouble, but Daniel would not do anything wrong.

Then the men had an idea. They went to King Darius.

"You are a great king!" they said. "Why don't you make a new law? For the next thirty days, no one may worship anyone but you. If they do, they will be thrown into a den of lions!"

The king made the law. But Daniel did not obey it. He worshiped God, just as he had always done. The bad men ran and told the king.

The king was sad. He liked Daniel, but he could not change the law.

So Daniel was taken to the lions' den. The lions had sharp teeth and claws. They were very hungry.

The king could not sleep that night. In the morning, he rushed to the lions' den. "Daniel?" he shouted.

Daniel replied, "The lions haven't hurt me! God sent an angel to shut their mouths."

King Darius was so happy he made a new law. "From now on, everyone must worship Daniel's God," he said.

> *Please, God, help me to be as brave as Daniel.*

49

Jonah Runs Away

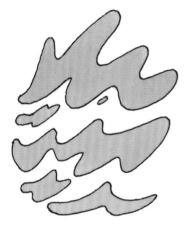

Jonah was a prophet. One day God came to him with a message.

"The people in Nineveh are wicked," said God. "Go to Nineveh and tell them to stop what they are doing, or I will punish them."

Jonah did not want to go to Nineveh. He decided to run away from God. He found a ship, paid his money, lay down in his bunk, and fell fast asleep.

When the ship set sail, God sent a storm. The wind blew strong, and the waves grew high. The ship went up, up, up and down, down, down.

The sailors were scared. "We're going to drown!" they cried.

They woke up Jonah. "Pray to your God!" they said. "Maybe he will save us."

But Jonah was running away from God. He did not want to pray. "This storm is my fault," he said. "You must throw me into the sea."

So the sailors threw Jonah overboard, and the storm stopped. Jonah began to sink. But God sent a huge fish, who swallowed up Jonah in one big gulp.

Inside the fish, Jonah had time to think. "I'm sorry!" he said to God. "I shouldn't have run away." Then the big fish swam near the shore and spit Jonah onto the sand.

"Go to Nineveh," said God. And this time Jonah went.

The people of Nineveh listened to God's message. They were sorry for the bad things they had done. And God forgave them.

Thank you for forgiving me when I am sorry.

Mary's Baby

Mary lived in the little village of Nazareth. She was planning to marry a carpenter named Joseph.

One day the angel Gabriel came to Mary.

"God is very pleased with you," said Gabriel. "You are going to have a baby. He will be called the Son of God. He will be a great king, like David."

Mary did not understand. But she knew the angel had come from God. "I will do whatever God wants," she said.

When Mary told Joseph what the angel had said, he

did not understand either. But one night the angel visited him too. "Don't be afraid," the angel said. "Mary will have a baby boy. You are to name him Jesus. He will save God's people from their sins."

The time came for the child to be born. Mary and Joseph had to travel to Bethlehem. It was a long way, and Mary was tired. She wanted to lie down and rest.

Joseph went to the inn and knocked on the door.

"Do you have a room?" he asked.

The innkeeper shook his head. The inn was full. The innkeeper saw how tired Mary was. "You may stay in the stable," he said.

So Mary and Joseph went into the stable. That night Mary's baby was born.

Mary gently wrapped baby Jesus in strips of cloth and laid him in a straw-filled manger.

Thank you, God, for baby Jesus.

The Angels and the Shepherds

It was midnight, and it was cold. Stars twinkled in the winter sky. Huddled around a fire, some shepherds tried to stay awake.

Suddenly a bright light shone all around them. The shepherds were frightened. What could this be?

A loud voice said, "Don't be afraid!"

The shepherds looked up into the sky and saw a bright, shining angel.

"God has sent me with good news for the whole world!" said the angel. "A baby has been born in Bethlehem. He will be your King and Savior. You will find the baby in Bethlehem asleep in a manger."

Suddenly the whole sky was filled with angels. They danced and sang, "Glory to God in the highest, and peace to all people on earth."

When the angels finished their song, the shepherds said to each other, "Let's go to Bethlehem and see what has happened!"

Through peaceful fields and quiet streets, they ran and ran. Soon they found the stable. They carefully pushed open the door.

The baby Jesus was asleep in the manger, just as the angel had said.

"This is the promised child," the shepherds said. And they told Mary and Joseph about the angels' song.

Glory to God in the highest, and peace to God's people on earth.

The Journey of the Wise Men

In a country far from Bethlehem, some wise men studied the sky. One night they saw a new star. It was bigger and brighter than the other stars.

"What does it mean?" one wise man asked.

"A king has been born!" said the second.

"Let's go find him," the third wise man said.

So the wise men set off on a long, long journey, following the star. At last they reached Jerusalem.

"Kings live in palaces," said one wise man. So they went to the palace where King Herod lived.

"We are looking for the new king," the wise men said. "Is he here?"

Herod was surprised. Then he got angry. He did not want a new king. He wanted to be king himself.

Herod said to the wise men, "Find out where the new king is. I want to go worship him."

The wise men left Jerusalem and followed the star. It led them to a little house in Bethlehem. There they found Mary and Jesus.

The wise men knelt down and gave Jesus presents of gold, frankincense, and myrrh.

That night the wise men learned that Herod wanted to hurt Jesus. "We must not tell Herod where Jesus is," they decided. "We must not go back to Jerusalem."

Dear God, help me to think of a gift to bring to Jesus.

The Four Fishermen

The Sea of Galilee was full of fish. Lots of fishermen worked there.

One day Jesus went for a walk by the Sea of Galilee. He saw some fishermen mending their nets. He saw others counting the fish they had caught.

Jesus saw a little fishing boat close to the shore. Two of his friends were in the boat. They were throwing their nets into the water, hoping to catch some fish.

"Peter!" Jesus called. "Andrew!"

The two brothers looked toward Jesus. "Come with me!" Jesus said. "I will teach you to catch people, not fish."

Peter and Andrew dropped their nets. They jumped out of their boat, swam to the shore, and followed Jesus.

Jesus kept walking. He saw two more brothers, James and John, sitting

Lord Jesus, I want to follow you.

58

in their fishing boat. They were getting their fishing nets ready.

"James!" Jesus called. "John!" The two men looked to see who was calling. "Come with me!" said Jesus.

James and John left their boat and went straight to Jesus.

The four fishermen became Jesus' first disciples. Everywhere Jesus went, they went too.

Jesus Meets Matthew

Matthew was a tax collector. He collected money for the government. He also collected a lot of extra money for himself.

Matthew was lonely. People didn't like him because he cheated them.

One day while Matthew was collecting money, he saw Jesus. "Matthew," Jesus said kindly. "Leave your work, and follow me."

Matthew was surprised. He did not expect Jesus to like him. "Will you eat with me at my house?" Matthew asked. "Come and bring your friends."

Jesus had dinner at Matthew's house. He brought Peter and Andrew and James and John.

Lots of tax collectors joined them. Other lonely people from the village came too. Jesus wanted to eat

with all of them.

Some men saw Jesus at Matthew's house. They didn't like Matthew, they didn't like the tax collectors, and they didn't like the lonely people.

The men went to Jesus' friends and asked, "Why does Jesus eat with tax collectors and lonely people?"

When Jesus heard what they were saying, he said to the men, "You have many friends, but these people are lonely. I came to be friends with the people who need me. God wants us all to be kind to lonely people."

Dear God, help me to be kind.

The Four Kind Friends

Lots of people went to see Jesus. Some wanted to hear him speak. Some wanted him to make them well.

One man could not go to Jesus. He could not walk. He could not sit up. He could not move at all. So he did not think he would ever see Jesus.

The man's friends had a good idea. They put him on a mat and carried him to the house where Jesus was staying. They were sure Jesus would make him well.

But when they got to the house, they saw people everywhere—in the house, in the yard, in the street. There was no room in the house for the man on the mat. His friends could not even see the door.

Then his friends had an idea. Outside the house were some steps going up the side of the house. Very carefully, they carried the man up the steps. Very quietly, they made a hole in the roof.

The people inside the house looked up as the four friends lowered the man on the mat into the room.

Jesus looked at the man lying on the mat. "Your sins are forgiven," said Jesus. "Stand up! Pick up your mat, and go home."

The man sat up. He stood up. He bent down and picked up his mat. The people in the house moved back so the man could walk out the door.

"We have never seen anything like this," they whispered to each other.

Then they all shouted, "Thanks be to God!"

Thank you for my friends.

The Story of the Two Houses

Once Jesus told a story about a wise man who wanted to build a house. "Where shall I build it?" the man wondered. "Shall I build it near the river? Shall I build it near the sea? Shall I build it in a field? No! I will build it on solid rock!"

The wise man began to build. He worked hard. He worked for a long time. When his house was finished, he was pleased.

Suddenly a terrible storm blew across the sea. The winds howled. The rain poured. The rivers grew higher and higher.

The wise man's house trembled and creaked. It

64

shivered and shook. But it did not fall down. It was built on strong rock.

There was also a foolish man who wanted to build a house. "I don't want to build on rock," he said to himself. "It is hard to build on rock. It takes too long. I will build my house on sand."

And so the foolish man built his house on sand. He built it quickly. It was not hard to do.

Then the storm came. The winds howled. The rain poured. The rivers grew higher and higher.

The foolish man's house trembled and creaked. It shivered and shook. It wibbled and wobbled. And suddenly it crashed to the ground. The foolish man's house fell down because it was built on sand.

"If you listen to me and do what I say," said Jesus, "you will be like the wise man who built his house on the rock."

Lord Jesus, help me to listen to you and to do what you say.

The Big Storm

Jesus and his disciples had spent the day by the Sea of Galilee. It was late, and they were tired. They wanted to go to a quiet place to rest.

"Let's cross the lake," Jesus said. He and his friends got into a boat. Jesus lay down, put his head on a pillow, and soon fell fast asleep.

While he slept, the winds began to blow. The waves crashed and the boat rocked. Up and down, higher and lower it went. The water splashed and smashed over the little boat's sides. It was going to sink!

Jesus' friends were frightened. They went to Jesus and shook him awake.

"Help!" they shouted. "We're going to drown!"
Jesus stood up.

"Be quiet!" he shouted to the wind. The wind stopped howling.

"Be still!" he shouted to the waves. The sea grew calm.

Jesus' friends didn't know what to say. First they were excited. Then they were afraid.

"He must be very important," they said to one another. "Even the wind and the waves do what he says!"

Thank you, Lord Jesus, that you are bigger and stronger than I am. Please help me when I am afraid.

The Girl Who Came Back to Life

Jairus was sad. His little girl was sick. The doctors thought she was going to die. "I will ask Jesus to help her," he said to himself.

Lots of people were trying to talk to Jesus. Jairus knew he did not have time to wait. He pushed through the crowd and knelt at Jesus' feet.

"Please come to my house," he begged. "My little girl is only twelve years old, and she is dying. Please help her."

Jesus followed Jairus. But they had not gone very far when they met a messenger from Jairus's house.

"It's too late," the messenger said

to Jairus. "Your little girl is dead."

Jairus began to cry. "Don't be afraid," Jesus said. "Have faith, and your little girl will be well."

When they got to the house, they heard many people crying loudly.

"There is no need to cry," Jesus said. "The little girl isn't dead. She is sleeping."

The people made fun of Jesus. They knew the little girl was dead. But Jesus went into the little girl's room anyway. He held her hand.

"Get up, little girl," he said.

The little girl woke up. She got out of bed. She walked around the room. "I'm hungry," she said.

"Go get her something to eat," Jesus said.

The little girl's parents could not believe their eyes.

Lord Jesus, I'm glad you help children.

The Living Bread

One day Jesus went into the countryside. A big crowd of people followed him. They all wanted to be with Jesus.

It was getting late, and Jesus knew that everyone was hungry. He went to his friend Philip and asked, "Where can we buy some food for these people?"

"For all these people?" Philip said. "We don't have enough money to feed this crowd!"

Jesus' friend Andrew brought a little boy to him. "This boy wants to give you his lunch," Andrew said, "but it won't do much good. He's only got five small barley rolls and two little fish."

Jesus smiled. "Tell everyone to sit down," he said.

Then Jesus took the lunch from the little boy. Jesus thanked God for the bread and fish. He gave the food to his friends. His friends gave it to the people sitting on the grass.

The more food they gave away, the more there was. Everyone began to eat. Everyone had more than enough.

Jesus told his friends to gather up the food that was left over. They filled up twelve big baskets.

Jesus told the people, "I am the living bread that came down from heaven. If you eat this bread, you will live forever. I will give my body for the life of the world."

The people wondered what Jesus meant.

Lord Jesus, you are the Bread of Life.

The Good Neighbor

Someone asked Jesus, "How can I be sure I will live with God forever?"

"Love God and love your neighbor," Jesus replied.

"But who is my neighbor?" the person asked.

So Jesus told a story about a man who went on a journey. Suddenly some robbers grabbed the man and knocked him to the ground. They took his clothes and ran away.

Soon a priest came down the road. He saw the man lying on the ground, but he did not want to help him. He crossed over to the other side of the road.

Then another man came down the road. He saw the man lying on the ground, and he too crossed over to the other side of the road.

Finally a man from Samaria came down the road. He saw the man lying on the ground, and he stopped to help.

The Samaritan bandaged up the man's wounds. He gently lifted him onto his donkey. He took him to the nearest inn.

"Please take care of him," he said to the innkeeper. "I

will pay for everything he needs."

Jesus turned to the man who had asked, "Who is my neighbor?" Jesus asked him, "Who was the good neighbor in that story?"

"The one who helped the wounded man," the man answered. "The one who was kind."

"Be like him," Jesus said.

Dear God, teach me to be a good neighbor.

The Story of the Lost Sheep

Jesus told a story about a shepherd to the people who came to listen to him.

The shepherd had a hundred sheep. Every day he counted them: "One, two, three, . . . ninety-eight, ninety-nine, one hundred." He knew them all. He loved them all.

One day the shepherd went to count his sheep: "One, two, three, . . . ninety-eight, ninety-nine . . ." But where was the hundredth sheep? It was missing!

The shepherd grabbed his staff and ran through the hills looking for the lost sheep. He looked in bushes and on rocky ledges. He looked in ditches and under trees. The shepherd looked everywhere. He did not give up.

Then the shepherd saw the lost sheep. He ran to rescue it. The sheep was happy to see the shepherd. The shepherd was even happier to see the sheep. He picked it up, put it on his shoulders, and carried it home.

"Look, everyone!" he said to his friends. "I've found my lost sheep. Let's have a party!"

His friends were happy because the shepherd had found his lost sheep.

Jesus looked at the people who were listening to him.

"God is like that shepherd," he said, "and some of you are like the lost sheep. God has come to rescue you. When he finds you, he is as happy as the shepherd who found his lost sheep."

The Lord is my shepherd.

The Man Who Could Not See

Bartimaeus was blind. He sat by the side of the road and held out his begging bowl as people walked by. Most people did not stop to talk with him.

One day Bartimaeus heard lots of footsteps. He heard people talking and laughing. Someone said, "Jesus is coming!"

Bartimaeus knew about Jesus. Jesus stopped storms. Jesus told people about God. Jesus helped people.

Bartimaeus shouted as loudly as he could, "Jesus! Help me!"

"Be quiet!" someone said.

"Jesus!" Bartimaeus shouted again.

"Stop shouting!" said someone else.

But Bartimaeus kept on shouting. He shouted so much that he didn't hear Jesus speaking.

"Tell Bartimaeus to come here," said Jesus.

"Jesus is asking for you," said a kind voice.

Bartimaeus threw off his cloak and leaped to his feet. He stretched out his arms and felt his way through the crowd.

"What do you want me to do for you?" Jesus asked.

"I want to see!" said Bartimaeus.

"You will see," said Jesus. "You believe that I can make you well, and so I will."

Suddenly Bartimaeus saw light. He saw colors. He saw people and houses and trees. And he saw Jesus. He had been healed!

Jesus kept walking, and Bartimaeus followed him down the road.

When I need help, Lord Jesus, remind me to ask you.

The Little Tax Collector

Zacchaeus was the chief tax collector in Jericho. He was very rich because he kept much of the money for himself. No one liked Zacchaeus. They called him a cheat.

One day Jesus went to Jericho. People pushed and shoved so they could get close to him. They stood on tiptoe and jumped up and down so they could see. But Zacchaeus was a short man, and he could not see Jesus.

Then Zacchaeus saw a sycamore tree, and he had an idea. He climbed the tree and sat in its branches. Now he could see everything. He could see Jesus walking toward him and talking to the people.

When Jesus reached the tree, he stopped walking.

Zacchaeus peeked through the leaves. Jesus was looking right at him.

"Zacchaeus," Jesus said, "come down quickly! I want to go to your house today."

Zacchaeus slid down the tree trunk and ran home. "Jesus is coming for dinner!" he shouted.

Now that Jesus was his friend, Zacchaeus did not

care about being rich. He did not want to cheat people anymore. "I'm sorry I was greedy," he told Jesus. "I will give half of my things to the poor, and I will repay all the money I have stolen."

"Good for you, Zacchaeus," said Jesus. "Now you are following me."

The King on a Donkey

It was Sunday, and Jesus and his disciples walked toward Jerusalem. As they got near the city, Jesus sent two of his friends to the next village to find a donkey.

When they brought Jesus the donkey, he climbed on its back and headed for the city.

Many other people were also on their way to Jerusalem. When they saw Jesus coming, some laid their coats on the road. Others spread out palm branches to make a path for the donkey.

80

As Jesus rode by, they shouted,
"Blessed is he who comes in the name of the Lord! Hosanna in the highest!"

That Sunday the people wanted Jesus to be their king. They did not know that on Thursday he would eat his last supper with his disciples.

"This is my body, which I will give up for you," he would say as he gave them bread.

"This is my blood, which I will shed for you," he would say as he gave them wine.

Even Jesus' friends did not know that he would die on Friday afternoon. But Jesus knew.

Hosanna in the highest!

Jesus Is Crucified

Jesus had enemies in Jerusalem. They did not like what he said about God. They wished he would stop healing people. They were angry because people paid more attention to him than to them.

Jesus' enemies thought of a way to get him in trouble. They told lies about him and had him arrested. Even though Jesus had done nothing wrong, the rulers of Jerusalem said he must die.

Soldiers dressed Jesus in a purple robe like a king. They made a crown for him out of thorns, and they jammed it on his head until blood ran down his face. They hit him and spat on him.

The soldiers put a heavy cross on Jesus' back and made him walk down a narrow street. The cross was so heavy that Jesus stumbled. He stumbled again. A man named Simon helped Jesus carry his cross.

When they came to Golgotha, the soldiers nailed Jesus to the cross and dropped it into the ground. Jesus' mother, Mary, and his disciple John waited near the cross. There was nothing else they could do.

Suddenly the earth shook and the sky turned black. Jesus cried out in a loud voice, "My God, my God, why have you forsaken me?"

And then he died.

"He really was the Son of God," said one of the soldiers.

Later that day, some friends put Jesus' body in a tomb. They rolled a big stone across the entrance. Then they went home and cried.

Oh, dear Jesus, I am so sad that you died. I love you very much.

83

Jesus Is Alive

On Friday afternoon, Jesus died.

All day Saturday, his friends talked about him and wept.

Very early Sunday morning, his friend Mary of Magdala decided to go to the tomb.

It was still dark when Mary arrived. But she could see that something had changed. The big stone had been rolled away from the entrance. The tomb was open.

Mary looked inside. The tomb was empty. Jesus was not there. Mary began to cry.

Suddenly she saw two angels. "Why are you crying?" they asked.

"They have taken Jesus away, and I don't know where they have put him," she cried.

Mary saw a man standing behind her. She thought it was the gardener. "If you have taken him, please tell me," she begged. "I will go and get him."

"Mary!" the man said.

Mary knew that voice. It wasn't the gardener. It was Jesus. He was alive!

"Go and tell my friends that I am alive!" Jesus said.

Mary ran to tell Jesus' friends the good news. "He is alive! I have seen him with my own eyes!"

Jesus, I am so happy you are alive now!

Thomas Believes

Everyone in Jerusalem knew the story. Jesus had died, but Jesus was alive again!

Most of Jesus' friends had seen him and talked with him. They had seen the marks on his hands and feet where the nails had been.

But Thomas had not seen Jesus. He did not believe that Jesus was alive.

He did not believe the other disciples. He did not believe the people who were talking about Jesus all over Jerusalem. He did not believe Mary of Magdala.

86

"Unless I see him and touch the nail marks myself, I will not believe!" Thomas insisted.

A week after Jesus rose from the dead, all his friends met in one room. Suddenly Jesus was in the room with them. "Peace be with you," he said. Then he turned to Thomas. He held out his hands.

"Come, Thomas," he said. "Touch my hands. Feel the holes where the nails went through."

Thomas looked at Jesus, and he believed. Jesus had died, and now he was alive again. Thomas knelt down in front of Jesus. "My Lord and my God!" he said.

I can't see you, Lord Jesus. Help me to believe in you anyway.

87

Breakfast on the Beach

One evening Peter and six of Jesus' other disciples went out on the Sea of Galilee to fish. They threw out their nets and waited. All night they waited, but they did not catch a single fish.

The fishermen were tired and disappointed. As they turned to go home, they saw a man on the shore.

"Have you caught anything?" he shouted.

"No!" they said.

"Throw your net on the right side of the boat," said the man. "Then you will catch some fish."

The disciples were too tired to argue. They did as the man said. Suddenly the net was bursting with fish.

Peter looked again at the man on the beach. "It's Jesus!" he cried. Peter jumped into the water and swam for shore.

The others followed him with the boat and the net full of fish.

Jesus was cooking some fish over a fire. He had some bread too.

Thank you, Lord Jesus, for feeding your little lambs.

"Bring me some of the fish you've just caught," said Jesus. "Let's have breakfast together."

After breakfast Jesus asked Peter, "Do you love me?"

"You know that I love you," Peter answered.

"Feed my lambs," Jesus said. "I want you to lead my people and take good care of them."

Jesus Goes to Heaven

For six wonderful weeks after his resurrection, Jesus and his disciples spent time together. He walked and talked with them. He shared bread and wine with them.

"I have to go away," Jesus told them, "but I will be with you forever." The disciples wondered what he meant.

"Tell the whole world about me," Jesus said. "Teach people how to follow me." The disciples wondered how they would do that.

"Wait in Jerusalem," Jesus said. "God will send a helper, the Holy Spirit, to make you strong. Then everyone in the whole world will hear about me."

One day Jesus and his disciples went out to a hillside to talk. While they were watching him, he was lifted up. A cloud came down and hid him.

Suddenly two angels stood beside them. "Why are you looking at the sky?" the angels asked. "Jesus has gone to heaven, but someday he will come back."

The disciples remembered what Jesus had said. So they went to Jerusalem and waited for God to send the Holy Spirit.

Christ has died, Christ is risen, Christ will come again.

The Good News of Jesus

On the day of Pentecost, Jesus' friends met together in a house in Jerusalem. Suddenly they heard a sound like a rushing wind. It filled the whole house. Then they saw flames, but there was no fire.

The Holy Spirit had come! Now the disciples weren't afraid anymore. They went out into the city to tell people about Jesus.

People from all over the world had come to Jerusalem for a feast. When the disciples started to speak, the visitors were amazed.

"We can understand what they are saying!" they said. "How can they speak so many different languages?"

Peter stood up and said, "God has done something wonderful today. He has given us the Holy Spirit, a sign that God is with us." And he told them that Jesus had died, was risen, and would come again.

"Can we follow Jesus too?" many people asked.

"Confess your sins and be baptized," Peter said, "and you too will receive the Holy Spirit."

Three thousand people were baptized that day. They shared with one another. They learned, prayed, and broke bread together. And every day more people joined them.

Soon Jesus had friends all over the world.

Come, Holy Spirit, and fill our hearts.